MY SON'S JOURNEY FROM HIS CABIN

BY JANE SPELLMAN
2011

MY SON'S JOURNEY FROM HIS CABIN

Chapter 1
THE BEGINNING

I tip my candle toward his and light mine from the one he is holding. It's Christmas Eve 2009, and the church is filled with families, friends, the singing of *Silent Night,* and an emerging candlelight glow throughout. My heart is filled with joy and gratitude to a God who has given His Son to save this sinful world and has let me have my son here next to me to light my candle.

How different this time would be without God's love, mercy and compassion on my son and our family. I promised God at that moment that I will tell this story of His miracle in our lives so others can know of His love and His willingness to give us such miracles whether we deserve them or not and when we ask for them. And asked for this one, I surely did.

It goes back almost a year in January when I found myself struggling more and more with Chad's drinking problem. I hated that sinking feeling I would feel when I would see his red pickup truck turning into our yard, or parked at our house when I came home from work. I would have that initial quick thought of "shall I pass by and wait for him to leave?" But I would resist that impulse and pull in to visit with him a bit, ask him how his day was, and wait for him to leave to go to his apartment. Our Lord asks us to love unconditionally. *"Be completely humble and gentle; be patient, bearing with one another with love. Make every effort to keep the unity of the Spirit through the bond of peace." Ephesians 4:2-3* But that isn't always easy when the person we love is caught up and captured in something so damaging and hurtful as alcohol addiction.

I struggle with my tendency to avoid what isn't pleasing to me. I didn't like these feelings that I was feeling of wanting to avoid my son. I love him dearly. I had been praying for Chad all along and asking for prayers from my different bible study and church groups, as well as my friends. But I was increasingly troubled in my concern for him and with my desire to avoid him. I asked God to help me understand my relationship with Chad and his addiction. And one January morning He gave me this poem:

MY SON'S CABIN
By Jane Spellman

I follow the path, it seems so wide.
There are bushes, flowers and prickles along the side.
How easy it is to pass along,
It makes you feel like you belong.

I saw the cabin back where I stood.
It's off in the distance amongst the wood.
I hesitate to make my way,
Should I wait for another day?

No, I'll see what I can do
To tell him what I know to be true.
It's hard to look from the outside in.
It seems sometimes like no one will win.

But then it isn't really winning at stake.
It's about what we do and choices we make.
It's not up to me to be making predictions,
Or judging and talking about addictions.

Though a mother can long for a change of heart,

And give some hope and a place to start.
But it needs to come from a place within him.
I'm approaching the cabin, but it looks so dim.

It's small and cozy with windows galore.
I wonder if I should just go up to the door.
Very hard for me to be that direct,
So I'll look through the windows, see what I detect.

Some windows are hazy and some are so clear.
I can see why someone could be satisfied here.
The rooms appear comfortable but something's not right.
It's not on the surface, perhaps out of sight.

My wide path goes around to the back through a gate.
The front one is narrow and definitely straight.
The front door doesn't seem to be used at all.
I wonder about that as I gaze at a wall.

The glass window is clear as I look in the room.
There is furniture, guitars, all he needs, I assume.
I like this window – all is well it appears;
Nothing to cause concern or awaken my fears.

I move to the next one that is hazy and dark.
There are bottles and glasses, and the room is so stark.
This is the room that bothers me so.
It's the one that makes me just want to go.

It's here that the future is stagnant and gray
While ambition and health are taken away.
But I'm locked on the outside with nowhere to turn
Unless I convince him just what he must learn.

God made it clear He is always on our side.
He told of the pathways both narrow and wide.
Christ said that the narrow would be hard to endure;

But that He would be there and knocking at the door.

So that is the path and the door in the front!
I'll tell him about it: I'll try to confront.
I'll tell him that Jesus is just outside that door.
He can be free from addiction and have life ever more.

Looking through the windows is no doubt where I'll stay.
But I'll pray to our Lord for His mercy each day.
My son is my treasure, and I pray that he'll say,
"Come in, Lord Jesus, and show me the way."

Looking back, I can see that this was God's first gift to me in the process of giving me understanding and then answering prayers. I made copies of the poem and shared it with everyone I could think of. If you have experienced the Holy Spirit and its grace, you will know that I had no control over this sharing. It just comes about and happens. Not of my doing or of my own power – but of His.

I had sent a copy to my church Monday Morning Bible Study's leader, LaVerne. She is always so encouraging to me, and I thought she would like it. She asked me if I would read it to our Monday morning women's Bible study group of more than twenty-five women. Of course I said yes….just another step in God's plan for my sharing and asking for prayers for Chad.

So I wrote a devotional that included the poem, and I read it on a Monday morning in the middle of March. We had been studying the Book of Romans which I can now see was also in God's plan.

Romans 8:31 said to me, *"He who did not spare his own Son, but gave him up for us all – how will he not also, along with him, graciously give us all things."* Just ask me….God was saying. I spoke in my devotional about Romans 9:15, *"For he says to Moses, 'I will have mercy on whom I have mercy, and I will have compassion on whom I have compassion.' It does not, therefore, depend on man's desire or effort, but on God's mercy."* That verse particularly struck me. It's not what I do, but trust in what God can do.

I felt the need to reach out even further, to let as many as possible know about this need for prayer for Chad. "Just ask me"…. I could feel God telling me…"have others ask me as well"… So ask I did.

It was July 12th and a Sunday night when Ken answered the phone with a call from the hospital saying not to worry….Chad was okay but had fallen in his room. What?! We didn't even know he was in the hospital. He had gone to the emergency room that morning with intense stomach pain that had apparently scared him enough that he drove himself to the Emergency Room. They had admitted him.

We had weekend guests who were leaving the next morning; so I excused myself and drove to the hospital to see him. He was in a room and seemed pretty good. He had a couple of scrapes on his leg where he had fallen trying to drag his intravenous contraption with him to the bathroom unassisted. He said he was tired but felt fine; so I left him as he drifted off to sleep.

Monday morning our guests left early, and I headed to Byfield Parish Church to help with the hospitality tent on the first morning of Vacation Bible School. I had signed up for that morning and joined four other women as we awaited the arrival of parents and children for the week's first day signup process. My mind was on Chad, and I told the others about what had happened and my concern for Chad. As I was leaving, LaVerne walked with me to my car. She prayed out loud as we walked that God would protect Chad, relieve my concerns, and that all would be well with him.

I was heading to work, but something pulled at me to first go to the hospital and see how Chad was doing. As I pulled into the hospital parking area, I could see Chad's pickup truck up against the curbing with a man I didn't recognize in the driver's seat. I thought that maybe one of his friends from work had come to pick up the truck and was having a problem with it. I quickly parked my car and headed over to the truck. It was a hospital security man; and I told him that it was my son's truck and asked if there was a problem. I could see that the left front tire and the rear left tire were up against the granite curb and totally flat.

He said that my son had checked himself out of the hospital and had hit the curb as he was exiting the parking lot. They had called a tow truck and were helping him call for a ride home. I told him that I would be that ride and asked to see him.

What I saw was a total shock. His skin and his eyes were a sickening yellow color, and he was in a very agitated state. He had signed himself out of the hospital and had evidently gotten in his truck and was in such a condition that he hit the curb. The flattening of the tires certainly ended that intended exit; and with God's certain help kept him from injuring anyone at the hospital or on the road, including himself.

He was in a wheelchair and said he needed a cigarette. I asked if it was okay if I wheeled him outside for one and to have an opportunity to talk with him. So out we went to a far off corner. I got a cigarette from his truck, and we waited for the tow truck to come. Out in the daylight, the shock of his coloring was frightening. I told him that he needed to check himself back into the hospital, that he was very sick, and that he needed help. He begged me to just take him home to "get a couple of things" and that he would come right back. I was guessing that he was needing a drink badly at this point since he had been in the hospital since the previous morning.

He tried to get to his feet to walk but couldn't. I continued to try to impress on him that he needed the help that only the hospital could provide. That I wouldn't be able to help him get into his apartment anyway in the condition he was in. The tow truck came, and I can still see in my mind's eye the two of us and the security guys watching as the truck was pulled onto the tow truck bed. I gave the driver my information and where to take the truck.

Once his "escape" had disappeared, Chad was more willing to go back into the Emergency Room with me. He agreed to get re-admitted. I waited until they had him all set and called his dad to tell him the situation. The Emergency Room attending physician said that Chad was showing acute liver failure; but because he was thirty-three years old, they could not keep him against his will. I told him of my fear that he would try to check out again with his need for alcohol and cigarettes. Because he could now be considered a danger to himself and others, the hospital agreed to restrict his ability to leave without my consent. His dad and stepmother arrived very shook up, and stayed with him while I headed to work. Having them there with him was such a relief.

God's hand was certainly in this by stopping his departure from the hospital with the flattening of the tires without hurting anyone; by bringing me there just when I was needed; and by providing the kind of help he needed at the medical facility. It was a most disturbing morning; and the picture of his condition, his actions, and the thoughts of what might have been continue to haunt me.

That evening when I went to visit him, I was somewhat surprised that they had a young lady sitting there in his room with him. It was apparently to keep an eye on him since he had become a bit more agitated. He was very sleepy and fell asleep while I was talking with him. He looked peaceful, so I went home knowing that he was getting help and was safe now,

On the third day, I witnessed the Devil in action. The situation had certainly changed over night. Chad's arms and legs were tethered to the bed, there was a young attendant sitting next to him, and Chad was spouting off abusive language and ranting and raving at her and anyone within his range. It was not my son there – it was clearly the Devil fighting to hold him in his power through his addiction. Such evil to witness, more than I could bear to see. I told the sweet young lady that this is not what my son is like, apologized for his abuse, and couldn't get out of there fast enough for me. There it was, plain and simple, the horror of addiction; and my son was in the middle of it.

When I went to visit him in the evening, he had been sedated to some extent; but he was still very difficult. The nurse in charge had been scratched by him and asked for my permission to have him tested for HIV as a matter of course. Again I apologized and tried to explain that the Chad she was experiencing wasn't who he really is. I could hear his ranting from the corridor and just couldn't bring myself to go in. The evil was repelling me – God was protecting me. I prayed that God would save him from this horror of alcohol withdrawal.

I was told before I left that they would be transferring Chad to the Critical Care Unit because they could not handle him on the floor he was on. He could be heavily sedated at that unit until he came out of the withdrawal. It was certainly understandable and a relief that he could be spared from experiencing this nightmare.

Chapter 2
CRITICAL CARE UNIT

It was Wednesday, July 15th, when I pushed the button outside the Critical Care Unit and waited to identify myself and to be let in to see Chad. There is no just walking in at any time to see a patient in this location. Only immediate family members are admitted and at the timing and discretion of the personnel. He was being worked on at that moment, so I was asked to wait. Soon I was admitted into the corridor through the automatic opening doors and made my way down to the private room where he was located.

Whose hands are these? And those huge puffy feet that are peaking out from under the stark white sheets – who do they belong to? There was certainly no resemblance here to my son who I just saw last night. He was filled with fluids from the failure of his liver, and his very breathing was taken over by the apparatus that was hanging from the corner of his mouth. There were monitors everywhere with numbers that meant nothing to me – but were alarming in their quantity and fluctuation.

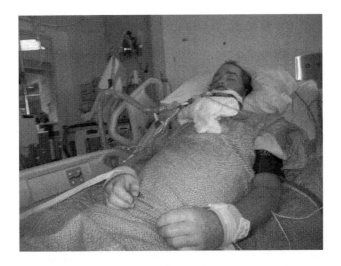

But for the first time, Chad was peaceful and unaware in a sedated state that is so deep that it is like a coma. I'm told that is why he is on the respirator. He would not be able to breathe on his own under this heavy sedation. The gift is that he will miss the alcohol withdrawal, and testing will be done to determine the extent of his liver damage.

His dad Peter and stepmother Jane were there as well, and we stood there looking at our son with

heavy hearts.   So many questions coming to mind:
What about all of this bloating?   How long will he
need this breathing apparatus?   Is his liver
damaged?   And the ultimate question – will he
live?

 Both Peter and Jane were red eyed and tear filled at
the sight of him, but tears don't come easily to me.
I found his peaceful sleeping reassuring.   All I
could see was his sweet face with those extremely
long eyelashes. He must have been teased about
those lashes at one point at a young age, because I
remember him coming home from elementary
school and cutting them short and close to his
eyelids.   They had grown back, and they brought
me comfort at this moment as I looked at his now
peaceful and handsome face.

We were told that they were monitoring his
condition and anticipated that it would be many
days before he could be brought out of this sedated
state. There would be no immediate change, and
they would be doing all they could to compensate
for the lack of function of his severely damaged
liver. I was expected at work and so left Peter and
Jane there as they tried to come to terms with this
turn of events.

The next days passed with little change in his
condition. They were draining the fluids from his
body and monitoring him constantly.   Peter and

Jane sat by his bed from mid morning until early evening each day and managed to get what information they could from the physicians and nurses coming in and out.

I had sent out an e-mail to my family and friends to tell them about what had happened and asking for their prayers. It all seemed so unreal and so horrible.

If I had any question of whether God was present in these beginning days, His presence was made know to me that Sunday when I went to church. "Amazing love, how can it be, that you my God would die for me".....the praise band was singing this song that never fails to move my heart and has special meaning for me. The tears I had not been shedding were streaming down my cheeks. All the tears that weren't shed this past week were coming now. It is not a praise song that they sing very often; in fact, it had been a very long time since they had. It was God telling me that He would be with me through this and with Chad. He was telling me that He is in control and to trust. Psalm 28:7 says, *"The LORD is my strength and my shield; my heart trusts in him and I am helped; my heart leaps for joy and I am helped."* Trust....not so easy when your son is so sick, and joy certainly wasn't what I was feeling at the time. But I came from church that morning knowing that God would be in control and with us through this.

That night I met the hospital chaplain while I was waiting to be let in to see Chad. We spoke briefly of Chad's condition, and I asked if he would look in on Chad and pray for him. He said he would. I once again felt God's hand in this and felt at peace. The next night, around 10:30 p.m., I was awakened by a phone call from a nurse at CCU. She said that Chad was experiencing bleeding from the esophagus, and they were seeking approval for the doctor to scope him and band the veins to stop the bleeding. She said I needed to understand that he might not make it through this procedure before giving my approval to proceed. I said that I understood and to do whatever they needed to do. She had another nurse come on to confirm my approval and said they would call back after the procedure to let me know how it went.

The wait for the call back seemed like forever; but it did arrive with the news that the banding was successful and that Chad was stable. What a relief that was, and I thanked God for his faithfulness to us and for guiding the doctor's hands to keep our son alive.

The next day, I contacted our church assistant pastor and asked if he would visit Chad and pray for him. Pastor Boylan was out of the country, but I knew that Pastor Dan would be willing to visit Chad and pray for him. He was kind enough after to e-

mail me about his visit with Chad and to tell me
what he prayed.

> *"Dear God, I thank you for Chad. I know*
> *You love him. You created him in Your*
> *image and created his soul out of nothing. I*
> *know You only do what pleases You (Psalm*
> *115:3), so I know you were pleased to make*
> *Chad. I know You love Chad. I pray that*
> *he knows that and loves You too through*
> *Jesus Christ. Lord, we have a lot of people*
> *praying for Chad and rooting for him. I*
> *don't know what the future holds, but You*
> *do. Reveal to Chad your love for him in*
> *Jesus and give him peace. Amen"*

It meant so much to me that Dan went to see Chad.
So many of my friends and church friends were
sending e-mails and cards to me with
encouragement and saying that they were praying
for Chad.

The same was true for Peter and Jane with their
friends and relatives. Jane's close friend Shirley
had contacted the Carmelite Sisters in Los Angeles
for prayers as well as the Carmelite Nuns in
Danvers. She said she asked for a daily rosary to be
said to include Chad, Jane and Peter. There were
so many prayers from such faithful followers and
friends. James 5:16 says, "*.....The prayer of the*

righteous man is powerful and effective." This certainly was our hope.

Chad's friend Jeff from middle school and high school also visited him and was praying for him. Jeff is a pastor of a church in Maine and had his church praying for Chad as well. God brought Jeff up from his own deep struggles and has done amazing work in his life. He is an example of how God can take a life and turn it around and use that life for His purpose. How I long for that for Chad.

It was hard for Chad's brother Jamie to be so far away in the State of Washington through all of this. We kept him informed about what was going on. But Jamie is a question kind of guy who would fire so many "what about this and what about that's" to me that it would make my head spin. We told him that it was very possible that Chad would not make it through this.

Jamie would send e-mails that he wanted me to read to Chad so that his younger brother would know how much he cared.

> *"Hi, Chad,*
>   *Wendy, Alexis and I have been getting multiple daily updates from Mom and Dad, and I want to let you know that I think of you all day. Today I took the day by myself to mountain bike around Mt. St.*

19

Helens. I went there today because this is where you and I went snowmobiling together a few years ago, and the mountain reminds me of you. I spoke to you a lot when I was there today…and prayed and prayed to be able to spend some quality time with you soon.

You are my brother, my blood, my family, and I love you tons. Dad or mom is reading this to you because I am waiting a couple of days until you are awake so I can fly there to see you and spend time with you. We have many things we as brothers need to do together, starting with the Yankees/Red Sox game the third week in August, just a few weeks away so get ready. I am 150% here to support you and help you in any way…We can fly to an island in the Caribbean until you heal or go fishing in Alaska…whatever you need!

We all take time and health for granted and yours isn't up yet! I have been so pleased to have such a good relationship with you. I enjoy more than anything, our time on the phone together, hearing about your karaoke nights and your amazing machining talents at work. You truly are a special talent and a special brother. You are really sick now, and I want you to focus on getting stronger

and healthier...I want to see you better soon.
You need to be strong and kick this thing
Think about how much you want to get out
of that hospital and back with your friends
and family.   I will be there with you!
I will see you soon.
                    Love, Jamie"

Jamie arrived a couple of days after this when Chad
had been taken off of the sedation.   He still was on
the respirator to breathe, but his alcohol withdrawal
was over and he was awake occasionally.   Because
of the toxins in his body from the failed liver, he
still had to have his hands restrained so that he
couldn't pull out the respirator and to stop him from
thrashing and trying to get out of the bed.

It was such a relief to me to have Jamie home and
also for his dad.   Jamie is a take charge person and
before long had all of Chad's monitor readings
figured out, knew all of the CCU doctors and
nurses, and was working on changing the rules of
visitation.

Not long after Jamie's arrival, I was buzzing into
the unit when the nurse said, "Well, he does already
have visitors; but you might as well join them."
When I went into the room, there were Jamie, Peter,
Jane, Chad's cousin Justin and his uncle Gerry all in
his room.   They had closed the curtain so that the
other visitors couldn't see the "exception" being

made for Chad.   So much for just one or two immediate family members at a time.

Jamie and his dad had gone out and bought a small DVD/CD player for Chad so he would have something to watch movies and play music for him with.   Jamie felt badly for Chad just lying there and wanted him to be stimulated to being more awake. He brought in Chad's *Grateful Dead* albums and instructed the nurses to play it for him during the night.   Justin had brought him the Seinfeld shows on DVD's to play for him.

Jamie was constantly looking to make Chad more comfortable.   He would shift him around in the bed, adjust his pillows, elevate the bed, and talk to him.   Whereas the rest of us would just sit and look sadly at Chad in the state he was in, Jamie wanted no part of that.   He went searching out doctors and nurses and questioned them on every facet of his health, he talked to him, and he looked for ways to help Chad communicate regardless of the fact that he had the respirator hanging out of his mouth.

Soon Chad was more alert and trying to communicate with us.   Jamie would get a piece of paper and a pen and put it in his hand to write something.   Chad couldn't control the pen very well, but he obviously wanted to make things known to us.   We considered getting a kids toy typewriter; but soon he was able to write a word here and there that we could grasp.

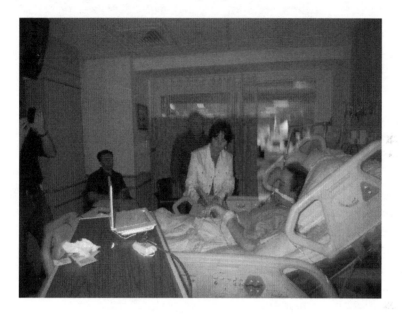

Jamie's time on his visit was devoted to Chad. While Chad was awake, he kept him entertained and comfortable; and when he was asleep, Jamie watched his numbers and checked with the doctors and nurses asking all kinds of questions. We decided to ask for a meeting with Chad's attending physician before Jamie went home. A meeting was set up for the next morning in the conference room outside of the CCU.

Jamie, Peter, Jane and I sat around a conference table with the doctor who had Chad's case for the past week as well as one of Chad's most attentive nurses Dan. Dan seemed to take a strong interest in Chad and his condition. He said it was partially because he was also 33 years old and was shocked at what Chad had done to himself with alcohol. I think that he could also see what a strong network of loving family that Chad had and how much we cared about him and loved him.

The doctor gave an overview of Chad's present condition. He said that his liver was in acute failure and showed a large portion of damage. He suspected that considering his condition and the abrupt and total failure that, along with the advanced cirrhosis, there was a definite possibility that there was also cancer. The only way to confirm this would be to take a biopsy which wasn't an option considering Chad's condition. He felt that Chad's only hope would be a liver transplant but explained to us that he would not even be eligible to get on a transplant list for six to nine months after being off of alcohol completely. He felt that Chad's prognosis was very poor.

As I listened to the doctor, all hope for Chad's recovery slipped away for me. I had listened to the facts; and even though it was heartbreaking, I was ready to accept what the doctor was saying would be the outcome for Chad. Not so with Chad's dad, stepmother or brother though; and I was amazed at that. Were they not hearing what I was hearing?

They were looking for ways to change the outcome while I was looking to accept the outcome.

I was ready to clean out Chad's apartment and look into getting a cemetery plot for him while Peter was asking how we could transport Chad to Lahey Burlington to meet with the Liver Specialist and Transplant Team that he had heard about there. They were looking for answers to get him better while I was trying to accept that this was how God would answer my prayers to save Chad from his life of addiction to alcohol. Not my desired outcome but trusting that it was God's will, which is not always in line with ours.

I wonder at myself sometimes. How was it possible that as a loving and devoted mother to her son, I was able to accept what was said while the others were not at all hearing or accepting it? I can only think that God has made that possible for me. He has given me the gift of inner peace and happiness even in the midst of trouble and sorrow, the ability to accept what happens, the ability to function in my daily life and face what needs to be done regardless of the situation. I wonder if it's the fact that I have welcomed Christ into my life and try to be and do what is pleasing to Him. Does the faith and trust that I have in Him give me the ability to cope while others around me don't see things in the same way? One of my favorite scriptures says, *"Do not be anxious about anything, but in everything, by prayer and petition, with thanksgiving, present your requests to God. And the peace of God, which transcends all understanding, will guard your hearts and your minds in Christ Jesus." ~ Philippians 4:6-7*   That is the peace that I'm talking about.

Meanwhile, the doctor said that Chad would need to get off of the ventilator soon.   They would look for an opportunity when his numbers seemed right for possibly supporting his breathing on his own.   The decision had to be made as to whether when it was removed to let him go if he could not breathe on his own or to put him back on life support possibly permanently.   We all agreed that Chad would not want to be kept alive under those conditions.   We would have to pray very hard that he would be able to breathe on his own.

Jamie reluctantly left to go back home on July 25th. His visit had a huge impact for all of us.   He brought an awakening to Chad through sheer determination and presence.   He had helped me move Chad's more valuable possessions out of his apartment and to our home.   And he had provided support to his dad and stepmother as well as to me that we really needed.   Jamie and Wendy had already planned to come to Ipswich the 20th of August on vacation.   We tried to think positively that Chad would be here at that time.

The gates of support were being opened to us. So many of my friends sent me notes of encouragement and even brought us meals. God has blessed me so much with supportive friends and family. It is in these hard times that such love is revealed and is treasured.

And Chad's friends and fellow workers were calling and concerned. Early in Chad's stay in the Critical Care Unit, one of the nurses said that someone was asking to come in who wasn't family. Jamie went out to see who it was and found Chad's friend Ed. Ed said that he figured he couldn't see Chad but that he just wanted to be near him because he was so worried. We told the desk to put Ed on the visitor list, and from that time Ed was a regular visitor to Chad.

On July 27th in the morning, we received a call that they had successfully removed the ventilator from Chad and that he was breathing well on his own with a slight assist from an oxygen mask. Chad could finally speak, although he was hard to understand at first. But even by that evening, we could understand him more clearly. It was a huge step for him, and his apparent comfort at not having it in his mouth was a relief to all of us.

Chapter 3
A BIT OF HOPE

Now that Chad was off of the ventilator and awake, the time was approaching when he would be moved from the Critical Care Unit back to one of the hospital floors. Seventeen days had passed since he first was put in the CCU, and the thought of him not having that degree of attention and care was a bit frightening. But it was understandable and certainly was an indication of some progress for him. On July 31st he said good bye to all those who had helped him so much and was moved to the sixth floor where he had been when he was first admitted.

Chad's condition had not improved much. His skin was jaundiced and he seemed to have a lot of confusion. Terrible colored fluids were still draining from his body. But he never complained of pain and discomfort. He watched TV and communicated a small amount but couldn't really carry on a conversation. It was heart wrenching to see him in this condition. He seemed to be slipping away.

He was able to have visitors now; and family, friends and fellow employees were stopping by to see him.   But they all felt they were saying good bye to Chad. No one could believe how awful he looked.   His condition was a shock to everyone who saw him.

The hospital social worker offered the services of Hospice.   I was in favor of meeting with them after experiencing the level of support that I had received with my caretaking of my mother. I think that Chad's dad saw it as giving up on him; but I convinced him to at least meet with the Hospice representative.   So we met with her on August 3rd to talk over options that Chad had at this point.   We ended up telling her that we would hold off for now. Peter was still hanging on the hope of getting Chad to the liver specialists at Lahey Burlington and looking at the liver transplant option.

The week ahead found Chad awake more and eating a small amount.   He slept a lot; but he also spent a fair amount of time watching TV and visiting with friends and family as they stopped by. He fortunately never complained of any pain.   Peter and Jane continued to spend a good portion of their days with him and made sure he was comfortable and had all of his needs met.

A report written by an in-hospital consultant who examined Chad on the 6th of August indicated the seriousness of Chad's condition at that point.   He stated that Chad appeared very debilitated and chronically ill, appearing older than his age. He was deeply jaundiced with very distended abdomen and extremities. His white blood count had been extremely high but appeared to be drifting downward. He showed advanced cirrhosis and end stage liver disease including ascites which is the presence of free fluid in the abdominal cavity and varices which is the bulging of veins which can bleed internally in the esophagus because of the weakened state of the blood vessels. The end of the doctor's report stated that Chad's prognosis seemed quite poor.

It was made evident to us that Chad could not remain indefinitely in the hospital and that we would need to start looking for outside of the hospital care for him. The social worker indicated that they would contact surrounding nursing homes and rehab facilities. Peter started the process of getting Chad on MassHealth coverage even though Chad's workplace had graciously indicated they would keep Chad on medical leave with their insurance coverage.

So often through those days, I would ask God to bring healing to Chad and to let me keep my boy. I was wrapped up in visiting him, keeping informed of his daily condition, talking with his doctors, cleaning out his apartment, and keeping family and friends informed of his condition. But this particular Sunday morning on August 9th, that verse from Romans Chapter 9, verse 15, came back to me and kept going through my head over and over. *"..... 'I will have mercy on whom I have mercy, and I will have compassion on whom I have compassion.' It does not, therefore, depend on man's desire or effort, but on God's mercy."*

I thought about that – it doesn't depend on what I want, or what Chad's dad wants in having him go to specialists, or even the kind of medical interventions at the hospital, but Chad was totally in the hands of a merciful and compassionate God. A God who I could turn to and who loves me and loves Chad even more than I can possibly love him. And the outcome for Chad was in God's hands. All I could ask for was His compassion and mercy that none of us deserve but that in His grace we so often receive. At that moment, I gave it up to Him with the realization that his compassion toward Chad might just be the release from a life of addiction through death as much as that answer would hurt more than anything. But also that God could have mercy on Chad through life. *"I will have mercy on whom I have mercy, and I will have compassion on whom I have compassion."* I could give up any control that I was seeking through my actions and the actions of others and pray for that mercy that was totally in God's hands. A feeling of comfort and peace flowed through me. I knew then that was to be my prayer.

Peter and Jane were visiting Chad when I went by at noon to see him. The gastro and liver specialist at the hospital came in while we were there. He had seen Chad from the very beginning and had always been kind and positive in speaking with us. He had told us not to give up on Chad. Well this day he said that Chad's liver had started to function and his numbers were improving. He had no explanation for this sudden change but it was apparent and encouraging.

We could barely believe our ears – this was the first real indication of hope. We left the hospital that afternoon elated and thrilled with the prospect of being able to give some good news to all of our family and friends. I could feel this journey taking a slightly new direction and it felt good. *'I will have mercy on whom I have mercy, and I will have compassion on whom I have compassion.'*

Chapter 4
COMING HOME

There was a definite change in Chad's condition
now. He was more alert and interested in eating.
Physical therapy sessions were put in place so that
he could get out of bed and start to walk. I went
out and bought flannel pants and T-shirts for him to
put on.

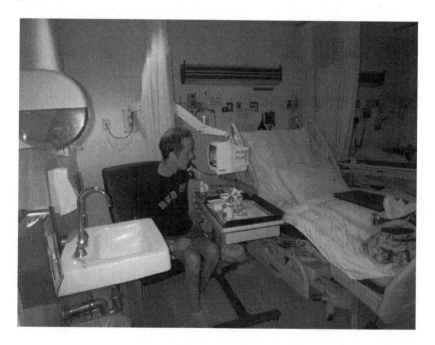

Each day brought continued improvement. He was able to get out of bed and walk with help to the bathroom. He had physical therapy most days and was getting slowly a bit stronger. He was no longer totally confined to his bed.

Food now had some appeal to him, and he would call us to bring him things like root beer floats and roast beef sandwiches when we came to visit. He was interacting with the nursing staff more and showed more interest in what was happening around him.

The social workers were talking more and more about his release from the hospital and into a facility where he could continue to rehab. They were not having any luck in finding a rehab facility within our area that was willing to take him, either because of his age and the nature of his illness or due to insurance coverage issues. We were informed by the hospital that Chad would need to be released from the hospital on August 18th. The social worker said that he was sure he could find a place for him to go by that date.

The reality of this impending future for Chad suddenly hit me. I could not imagine him in such a place. I thought about how he would hate that and how hopeless such a situation would be for him mentally when he was just starting to improve and come to life again. I knew in my heart that this just couldn't happen. That evening I spoke with Ken about the possibility of bringing Chad home with us. He said he also knew we couldn't consider any other possibility and that he had expected that would be what I would want to do.

I couldn't wait to get to the hospital the next morning to tell him. And when I did ask him if he would like to come to live at our house, the smile on his face and relief in his eyes told me that this was the only right alternative for Chad. I had been totally unaware that this decision would be made by me; but when I told my family and friends, they didn't seem surprised at all. Why is it that what is right to do sometimes just drifts above your head unrecognized? But when it does hit you square on, you know it's completely right.

I knew that Chad's condition would be challenging at home. I also knew that nursing services would be set up for him and that I wouldn't be taking it on alone. Ken is always supportive; and Chad's dad and stepmother would continue to be involved and help me in any way that I needed. There was no doubt that we could do this and help Chad get better in a place where he would be comfortable and completely loved and cared for.

Going home day came on August 18th as planned. Peter, Jane and I got to the hospital around noon. We were told that Chad had taken a fall the evening before and lacerated his tailbone. They had dressed the wound and included bandages and ointment that I would need. The issue with this wound was that Chad's system did not have the ability to heal normally. Little did I know at the time how true this would be. The attending nurse said that he couldn't sleep that night thinking about it which struck me as odd since it didn't seem like such a big deal to me. The main thing was that our son was going home.

Peter said they would meet us at home to help get Chad up the stairs to his new bedroom. Chad said he had one request on the way home. He wanted to get Kentucky fried chicken with mashed potatoes and biscuits. So off we headed to Danvers to get him his heart's desire – fast food! Yes, this boy was definitely getting better! Thank you, Lord.

The stairs were a definite problem for Chad. He had very little muscle at this point and very little fat on his body. He had no strength in his arms or his legs and had to be totally assisted, almost carried, up the stairs. Once he was up there, he had to remain. Fortunately, the bedroom is also adjacent to another big room so he had a large comfortable area.

Chad had dinner that first night in his room with his dad and stepmother who brought his dinner from their favorite restaurant. He was weak and tired, but very happy to be home. But at home we were on our own without the constant nursing and doctor care, and this was very scary.

It seems that God had prepared me for this time of caretaking of Chad. Although I am in my mid sixties, I am in better shape physically than I have ever been. Particularly this summer and fall of Chad's illness, I was working out at the YMCA with a personal trainer, walking with my sister-in-law three mornings a week, and doing a dog walking job for an hour a day seven days a week. This made it possible for me to lift Chad and help him move when needed and to go up and down the stairs many, many times daily.

My sister-in-law Donna told me about a story book character called Nurse Jane Fuzzy Wuzzy, and I took that name on myself. So, here I was being the very best nurse that I could be for Chad. And at this point, he certainly needed my help.

He was not strong enough to stand up from the bed. So his dad blocked the bed up high enough so he was able to get up from it with less assistance. Everything had to be adapted in this way. If he slipped down on the bed, I had to get from behind and pull him up. He had no strength at all. He needed help to do anything that involved movement.

The injury on his butt was proving to be a real problem. It was a big open sore that was very painful for him. It required new dressing often and just was not healing. I got a padded mattress cover which softened the bed and made it more comfortable; but Chad had to lie on his side was not able to sit on a chair. This confined him to the bed.

Visiting nurses had been set up for him as well as physical therapy three days a week. The nurses were able to monitor his condition and keep an eye on the sore which was very reassuring for me. And the physical therapist that was assigned to Chad is a very dear friend of mine who is a member of the Wednesday morning Bible study and prayer group that I attend. God certainly had a hand in this since she was someone I could fully trust and could voice my concerns to. And Patty had been praying for Chad all along.

Peter retrofitted the shower with a new shower head and handles; and he and Jamie had put the guest room together with Chad's TV and stereo system in place. We put Chad's dorm sized refrigerator in the room so he could have drinks and food available when he wanted it. I put up a bulletin board that had the cards and notes all attached so he could know how much he was thought of loved by everyone.

Jamie and Wendy arrived on the 20th of August for their scheduled vacation. And what a huge help and encouragement they were. They helped Chad fix up his room so he wouldn't be bored. The big room next to his was organized and cleaned out so Chad had plenty of space to walk around and have guests if he wanted. And with Jamie and Wendy's help we were able to finish clearing out Chad's apartment before the first of September. They spent lots of their Ipswich vacation time visiting with Chad and encouraging him. I was so grateful for their visit and hated it when it was time for them to head back to the West Coast.

Chad's progress in getting around continued to be quite slow, but he was gradually getting stronger. A big goal was to be able to go down and up the flight of stairs. And he worked hard to make that happen. He could get down the stairs fairly well, but he needed to be practically lifted to get up each stair going up. I was able to manage that with him. So we soon were able to at least go for rides and get out.

I loved that time with Chad. We would go for lunch or for an ice cream and just take a long ride up toward Newburyport and on the roads through the marshes. He was so grateful to be out of the house and such a pleasure to be with. And when we got back to the house, each time going up the stairs became easier for him.

Labor Day, September 7th, Chad went up and down the stairs and out of the house several times. Ed took him for a ride, his dad and stepmother took him out, and he wanted me to take him for an ice cream. He suddenly felt like he was making progress and had the freedom to go places when he wanted to.

The next afternoon we went for a follow up appointment with his doctor who told him how pleased he was with Chad's progress and how improved he was since he had last seen him. It was very encouraging.

But that evening, Chad said he really didn't feel all that well. His stomach seemed a bit upset. He didn't feel much like getting up or eating anything. He told me that he had thrown up. We figured it was something that he had eaten that didn't agree with him.

Later that evening he called me and had thrown again. I emptied and cleaned the bucket which had dark colored vomit and tucked him back in bed. It is hard for me to even write about that night because my stupidity still screams at me. I don't know what I was thinking – the fact was that I wasn't thinking. I was reacting to his needs and continuing to care for him. Nurse Jane Fuzzy Wuzzy….that was me – helping Chad when he couldn't get back in the bed when he was on the floor from trying to use the commode, lifting him back into bed, cleaning him up and comforting him.

I never woke Ken in the night or told him what was happening, I never called for help even when I should have recognized the signs that Chad was in trouble. It wasn't until after Ken had gone to work and I had managed to get Chad onto the commode that it all of a sudden was obvious to me that Chad was going unconscious and I needed to get help. I reached for the phone and called 911.

The ambulance arrived and the paramedics and firefighters got him down the stairs and whisked him off to the hospital. It was just in time since he had lost a lot of blood with internal bleeding. His blood pressure had dropped dangerously low and it was touch and go with him in the emergency room while they managed to band the bleeding blood vessels in his esophagus and replace the quarts of blood that he had lost.

He was placed back in the Critical Care Unit on September 9th. He had a very close call with death once again. And this time it was me who felt responsible. I had not cried before except that time in church; but this time I could not stop crying. I felt totally responsible for the situation getting to where it did. What was I thinking! How could I have let this happen?

41

I asked God why I had fallen so short in my care of Chad that night. My heart was broken and I felt so responsible. I found the following verse which said to me that from now on I needed to pray for God's wisdom and help in my caring for Chad. *"If any of you lacks wisdom, he should ask God, who gives generously to all without finding fault, and it will be given to him." James 1:5*

When Chad came home again, I needed to seek God's wisdom daily in his care, and I promised myself that I would do that. I would put aside my self blame, learn from my mistakes, and just look forward to his recovery from this setback with hope.

Chapter 5
BACK IN THE HOSPITAL

Chad was back where he started in the Critical Care Unit, but this time he had full knowledge of the experience. He pushed for the physical therapy that he now knew would make him stronger and able to get out of the hospital sooner. He was restless and impatient. But he was also very weak and ill and needed to be under the constant monitoring and care of the CCU.

One of the doctors who had attended Chad the first time had predicted that Chad would be constantly in and out of the hospital if he even made it. Those words went through my head now; but she didn't know our son's determination, and she didn't know that God was surely on our side. Chad was on a journey – a journey forward from his life of alcohol addiction; and even though this was a giant step back, I was confident that he would recover and move forward again.

A week passed under the care of CCU before he was released back to the same floor where he had been before. He was placed in the same room and reacquainted himself with the staff he had left only a month before. He was anxious to make this stay a short one and put his whole effort into the physical therapy offered.

His 34th birthday was approaching, and Chad was aiming toward spending it at home. He had a lot of convincing to do; but we told the hospital that we had all of the care and setup needed for his rehabilitation already in place at home. And I had certainly learned my lesson regarding getting help when I needed it – even if it was the middle of the night!

Chapter 6
HOME AGAIN

We checked Chad out of the hospital on his birthday on September 19th. His breakfast at the hospital was served on a birthday placemat, and the floor nurses and attendants all came by to wish him well and a very happy birthday. I needed assistance getting Chad into the car and up to his room at home; but we managed with his dad's help. It was a very happy and relieved guy who settled back into his room.

It was a different Chad who came home from the hospital this time. He had tasted the freedom of being able to get out and about, and he was determined to get that back and even more. He wanted no part of ever going back into the hospital. Patty commented on the difference in him during their physical therapy sessions. He was more outgoing and friendly – and much more focused on working on the exercises. Every day he was showing improvement and getting stronger.

It was decided that his red truck just had to go. It was a symbol of his past; and, truthfully, I hated the sight of it. I even had it put behind the garage out of my view. Chad's dad told him he would help him get a new truck and worked at getting the old one cleaned up and ready to sell.

We placed it out in front of the house with a for sale sign; and in late September, a couple and their son bought it as his first vehicle after getting his license. He had worked all summer earning money pulling lobster traps in order to get a pickup truck to haul his traps. It was the perfect truck for him. I said a prayer for the young man as they took it away for his continued safety in driving that truck and that he experience God's protection in it as Chad certainly had. It was one more step in Chad's journey forward.

Looking for a truck to buy gave Chad a whole new focus. He went to dealerships with anyone who would take him. He collected information, and we searched on my computer for models of pickup trucks that suited him.

He found a 2009 Ford Ranger pickup truck at a
Ford dealership in Portsmouth, New Hampshire;
and with help from his dad and a car loan; he was
able to drive it home on October 18. What a long
way he had come to be able to walk and drive a
truck just a month after getting out of the hospital.
It gave him a new freedom. I worried about that a
bit. He now had the opportunity to make choices
that previously were kept from. He could drive to a
liquor store and he could purchase cigarettes. But
he had no desire to do either.

Chad's desire for alcohol had been lifted from him.
So many people had said that he would need to go
into rehab or to AA meetings in order to get enough
support to keep him from drinking. But Chad

wasn't feeling this at all. He said he had
experienced the worst and he had no desire to go
back there. The desire for cigarettes was pulling at
him occasionally; but he said all he had to do was
look at the price and then look at his new truck and
he was able to overcome that.

He had set a goal of going back to work the middle
of November. It was hard to believe that he could
become healthy enough and strong enough to
resume his machinist job this soon. But he was
determined to make it happen. He just wanted to
get his life under control and get back to work.
Besides – he had truck payments to make!

Chad's health did continue to improve. His doctor
even commented during one examination that the
area of the liver seemed to have increased when he
compressed on his stomach. It certainly appeared
that way. He seemed to feel so good. His strength
was increasing daily, and his body seemed to fight
off infections and heal. His blood work showed
marked improvement. And he was gaining back
some of the weight he had lost.

Chad went back to work on November 19th just as
he had planned. I couldn't imagine that he could
start off full time, but he did. His fellow
employees were amazed and very pleased to have
him back at work. Many of them had visited Chad
in the hospital and did not expect him to survive.

To have him back at work and in apparent improving health was amazing. Before long he was not only working full time, but also working overtime.

Christmas time rolled around, and this was a particularly special Christmas for us to have Chad with us and to have his health so improved. One of his best gifts was an iPod Touch given to him by his brother and dad. In spite of never having any interest in computers before, he had it figured out and operating in no time. The iPod Touch opened the world of computers and cyberspace for Chad. It revealed an ability and interest that he didn't have before.

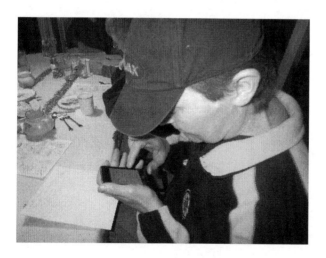

The greatest gift for all of us was to have Chad still with us. He would be heading into the year ahead without the burden of alcohol and nicotine

Yes, my candle was lit by his candle at the Christmas Eve service. Chad's journey is moving forward. It's exciting to watch. I am so proud of him and his determination not to drink or smoke and to have the quality of life that he has never experienced before. Addiction had stolen his life and kept him from his full potential. Now he certainly has a chance and a choice and a future.

Chapter 7
A YEAR LATER

As I look at Chad this year later and see the change
in him and the hope that he has for both his present
and his future, I have to ask why did God bring this
about for us? It was certainly not a matter of being
deserved – because nothing we do is deserving of
the mercy and compassion that God has shown us.
It certainly is nothing that I did even though I asked
God in prayer for Chad's deliverance from his
addictions and asked others to do so as well. It is
certainly not about me…nothing that I can do, ask
for, or am, is worthy of God's love for me.
Perhaps God has a plan for Chad's life, a plan that
will bring good, a plan that will reflect the grace of
God for others to see. Chad has been a testimony to
the ability to survive the effects of alcohol abuse, to
face whatever health issues arise as a result, and to
his continued choice to be free from his addictions
to both alcohol and nicotine this past year.

God has a plan for each of us; but whether we
follow through, seek His plan, accept His guidance
in reaching our potential by knowing Him through
His Word and then acting on it is totally up to us.
And this, of course, will be up to Chad. But I have
hope, and I have my son, and my heart is full of
gratitude.

"I know the plans I have for you, declares the LORD. Plans to prosper you and not to harm you. Plans to give you hope and a future."

Jeremiah 29:11

There will be those who will read this and see Chad's recovery in light of a medical success. But others like me will recognize God's incredible love shown in His mercy and compassion and know that it was truly a miracle. My prayer is that Chad's second chance and where it came from will be realized by him, and that he will eventually make a choice to seek Christ as his personal savior by opening that door that was always at his cabin of addiction but was closed. I pray that he will choose to open that door. And also for those who do not know of this opportunity through belief in God's Son that they will also open that door and let Christ into their lives. *"For God so loved the world that he gave his one and only Son, that whoever believes in him shall not perish but have eternal life."* John 3:16

What a journey we've been on this past year – and what amazing love we have experienced - all by God's grace.

> *"..... 'I will have mercy on whom I have mercy, and I will have compassion on whom I have compassion.' It does not, therefore, depend on man's desire or effort, but on God's mercy."*

With love in Christ,

Jane H. Spellman
Ipswich, Massachusetts

53

Made in the USA
Middletown, DE
22 August 2018